THE GATES

PURE LANGUAGE, AND OTHER EXCESSES

B. DOUGLAS KELLY

CONTENTS

ISBN: 978-1-953512-11-6 (Paperback)

ISBN: 978-1-953512-10-9 (eBook)

Front cover image owned by B. Douglas Kelly

Interior Formatting by C.E. Higgins

Print Copy by Truth Changes Media Press, in the United States of America.

First printing edition 2022.

Any references to historical events, real people, or real places are used fictitiously. Names, characters, and places are products of the author's imagination.

"The future is ugly because there is no unity, only ever deepening discord"

- From the Afterduction

For, who knows, the future, my children, you two.

To my mother, fellow poet, on a journey, who helped edit.

PART ONE
THE GATES

FOLLOW IT

I am no guru savant,

no jazzy hip-hop remote control bebopper of the whole Internet age
gone awry.
You won't find danceclub scenes
and lean chocolate cola-drinking rave fans of archaic drug-controlled
coded landscapes here.
No wet your whistle legpumping forty-year-old teens
incensed by tight-thighed liposuction fantasies
and gun-filled hate wars laughed at in high school homerooms.
We'll have none of this here.

No uplinks and offloads to escape from,
no wild money-crashing laughter streaming down alleyways
where cyberpunks database the elections away from square-jawed local
politicians
who are too busy anyway hiding from the big national camera focus
so they can swivel a hand up the skirts of younger lovers
with promises of riches and fastbucks.
Gone are those days.

No thought machine enhanced programs on sale to boast company
moral
by teamcreating rah-rah sections on workgroup chatsites.

Welcome to the free flow of language.

This is where the life occurs,
in form and function
where meaning is meant to be created
from what is stirred in the soul's darkness
by the language that moves inside.

Don't dream here mister.
Never anything for a buck.
Streamline that economic voodoo and let your impulse ride.

THE COMMAND

No time to reflect on some dread begotten night
hunched over family burning thoughts of outraged childhood memoirs.
No time to lay your stride in sync
with some medieval realm where smells of dragons
leave the 21st century a rambling pack of memories and madmen.
Gone are these days.
The sounds of now are to scream your madness out,
shake out your dreamkissing boots,
and Go.

Ramble down the open-ended highway of mad delights
the sense-mind has for sale;
jump in the digital bandwagon and humsing the theme song
of uncreated cinema dreams from the festering sores
on the thighs of Hollywood moguls that will make you dance with
    appreciation
for all the hate you've left behind.
There are no free thoughts
when the electric engine internet rumbles its naught plus one.
There are no open-ended questions in the valley of dying sunlight
    webshots.
There are no easy-paying easy-laying hookergirls
without graphic scenes of childhood rapes up for sale

on their imagined website real estate.
There's just the frenzy of you and me,
and every live wire connected between us.

And what we have left in our pocket
is the remnants of hope for an unmoving time,
feigned peace and the forgotten price of teenhood non-happenings:
whatsuch kisses and handholding sunsets,
first loves and broken hurt words filled with sharp spite
that we want to feel again and again.
But jump.
The wire is hot.
No reason to dull the senses when the final word of life is Go.

SONS OF PIONEERS

Make no mistake. I am night.

Born on the thick dark soul of millionaires,
sons of pioneers ready to take land and squeeze out markets,
I move out into the dreamland and fantasy life of teens with credit
cards,
deep in the self that seeps through our life views,
entering the tunnels of arteries to our heart,
racing through our brainblood vessels,
supplying oxygen and coin change,
causing headaches.

The pulsepounding sidewalks and cement dark streets,
the opalescent club queens and hitchhikers,
the fabulous driveways and gutters near the factory men,
pounding on our temples,
full of trash and spew,
soil dark dirt like blood
filled with cokedust and sugarsoda
and caffeine all-night studyfests and music shaking rhythms—
notes of the human body,
causing headaches.

If your head is aching, then this is the why:
the rhythm of America cannot leave you.
Your feet are pain bricks and twist backwards,
your hands computercramped and contorted,
your bowels twitching in lifeless suspension
like a toilet forever flushing and bubbling with gas.
The journey of moneylife is upon you.
The ka-ching of cashregisters is the lotteryticket rags-to-riches story,
immigrating upward to your pulsating heartmuscle walls.
America is descended upon you.

My life is the night now.
This electric light-heart movement glides me over the streets
and is burning itself bright in my heart,
like schoolchildren playground bound.
If I do not live on these aircushioned streets of Las Vegas
and scream my cash into a roulette hole,
then I am not here with you here in-country.
This is the real power:
the edge-filled moments of strangers shivering in rage
from stolen parking spaces.
The chips are uncounted and forever going down,
feel it, the clock ticking,
fill up the tank and head outwards to every god-knows-where side street
that turns into an open highway lined with hard-liquor disco diners.
You are full of money.
Your head is aching to expand.
Roll, roll, roll.

Ka-ching.

EURO-WORLD

There is a thick dark euro spine in the backbone of death.

A cold tea, a rotten corpse, a smiling child
and everybody rushing through the trains
in to the great known spaces of work,
cigarettes, burnt-out castles, too-remembered loves,
and every etcetera thrown in at the mindedge for safety and comfort.

More than dark is the great unfolding.
Never anywhere closer or more persistent.
Never anywhere greater or less interesting either.
Hopelessly bond, we move on together in mass,
desperately alone,
and hopefully never to be found.
This the world of gray absolute and heldfast promises,
or spirited interruptions where digressions are deliberately aimed
to circle back on target to the original subject conversations,
where breaths are held
and the dramatic effect only lowers the blood pulse.
Euro-dreams are made to come to life or come true,
there's no mickey mouse song singing here;
they are made to provide small lights to already suffering and snuffed
out beliefs.

Bigger words are grander thoughts here,
and dried up actions make the real world in the wetbrain no smaller.
The move-always inner worldlife
postures on the street corners
and sells itself to any passerby with a fifty franc bill
and an in-house dream of legspread marital bliss.
Back-to-back actions bring the future no clearer,
and forward we thrust out into emptyblack
and make the whole world bloom with a great and smiling decay.

Time is seeping away from us.
Grab on to any golden-shoed prostitute with a dissertation
and a dream of conquering bacteria
and get out there into the desert beyond the oasis.
Madness was made to be unfathomable,
and the horse rider with the six-shooters with dead bodies all around
is a safe explorer of the withered American nightmare that is not ours,
desiccated without a sense of love.

There's a great French authorname on the tongue,
and a blinding fist pounding in the air from the chant
and unaggravated revelry.
All sacred memories are unmeant and unkempt.
With foreign fires at border crossings unchecked
and restrained purchases on major items in place,
the network of trains run out into the night,
capturing stray students,
dominatrixes floating off to whipping parties,
and the sure-fire dreams of all factory workers
with state paid pensions fueling edge-city garden plots
and Italian beach getaways.

No mindset of nevermore and burning flames exist,
no mass-market schemes of endless expansion worldwide
with package delivery systems jumping over boarders exist.
Machines churn out unquiet angst
to drop high-end only consumer goods into display windows
dressed up for the weekend couple
when the small shop is closed to glaze their eyes with.

Europe World is the organized concrete safety net
is has quieted down to be.
The raging fires of empires are far behind it,
the briefcase carrying sports gangs
are on the way to collapse stadium fences and pelt police with rocks.
But we, we fly off from there.
We are America.

And we will get beyond it.

AT THE GATES

Stumbled,
in the land of the freaks

and the blind-hearted beggars grabbing the hungercrave
from wayward passengers departing
bus terminals and overzealous airports.

Out into the world.
Wherever there is a curve of understanding
in the lifelines of the geeks and corporate raiders,

the huddled-up immigrant taxi drivers
and the guitar-strumming trainwreck emergency crews
waiting by the water coolers in unanxious finger twitching,

there is the dream of life going on unending
in the island palmtree death in the forever hereafter.

Catch it here between hello-goodbyes of cola purchases
in international airports and at the gates
of on-ramps to major interstates.

We are all humbled and waiting at the gates.

And what better way to take advantage of this
then to clutter together in the boardrooms

to decide on consumer color patterns,

to mumble words in the clear silence around the base
of city-street garbage cans after all-night disco parties,

to master clichéd phrases to exchange in gentlemen's meetings
about inside trading and white-collar jury rigging.

No cynicism raps your knuckles here,
no cruel schoolteacher reality is staring at your inner sanctum
to understand the lack of pessimism and optimism
in this language riverflow melting around you,

no final act of betrayal from a thought long hidden or suppressed
can ride along this current wire of language

that contains the freedom of itself and for itself.

We are exercising away from that dark-light domain of pure judgment,
and hitting the random life meaning that hits us in parkingfields

after the theater lets out and the cocktails consumed,
that pours endlessly in our eyes and ears
and fills our bellies before we can digest it.

To get a sense of what lies outside the eye range of living is all we are
after.

A taste of the lack.

To get one slight opening crack,
a quiver, a hint, a slight breeze on the back of the neck in winter,

more than just standing at the gates.

This is why we hear it ring out: Go.

This is the command you've heard:
Burn fast and bright, and leave no trail behind you.

But this here is where we will always be:
humbled,
and waiting at the Gates.

PART TWO
AFTERDUCTION

A MUDDLED BACKGROUND

[I'm putting this introduction at the end. Poetry should be sensed and felt, not pre-interpreted to shade or inhibit any sensations, ideas, reactions that you get. To me, the sound is the sensation that drives the meaning.]

I wanted it all and yet be left at the end with just the haunting, the haunting of life. So, I had to stick with the full title in end. I can't get rid anything. They are just scarps that have clung to my flesh for so long, like washable tattoos or sticker price tags stuck to the bottom of my shoe: The Gates: The Book of the Poem; Pure Language and Other Excesses. The phrases are decades apart though.

In the beginning, back at the turn of the millennium, year two thousand, and the following year, I followed something I was told to call Pure Language. Draft chunks tumbled out. Well-formed utterances that slide out and had a sense but no form, at least no concrete discernible meaning to conceptually lock in place. Language just wanted to be. Like headless snakes coming out from rain gutters in the night when no one is around, the world is asleep in the suburb. They wanted only to move, and from their moving is their being. Do not disturb, encounter no one who could grasp them, catch them, tame them. The movement is their pleasure, their life, and before sunrise they have gone back down in their sewers, the storm drain, off into some resembling sleep no one can see. Meaning should not have humanity to guide it. It goes in its own direction.

That is what the sense of pure language was to me, a cadence in the brain before thought comes up, words are stuck to it, and we control it. It has its own shapes, pre-word, but whose undulations like the moving night snake on the street has movement, textures glistening in the moonlight; it knows what it is before words adhere to its scales. It is Pure Language, something primal. Our words are a burden to it. Our meaning, imposed.

This was first incarnation. Over the years I would return to listen, just to listen to it. There were then a few adjustments, some small changes subtly happening over time. Then finally, after a decade and a half or slightly more, a shaping into form. It now wanted to look like a poem, not like loose paragraphs. It was ready and safe to appear in final form. I knew, I knew when reading it was sounds, it was meant to be read out loud, quietly, when alone, or, better, mumbled in the mouth. Poetry must be first sound, that is what poetry has meant to be, *not* didactic, not diatribe, not clarity of moral judgement or even deliberate obfuscation. Not any of that. If you already know, there's no sense in discovering.

Those things come later, in the logic mind, post words. It must be a jangling of sounds in tempofalls, some mysterious rhythm flow, that might have meaning if you dig enough, chant enough, feel it in new ways. Or might not, and move on without you. Polemical and rhetorical it is not.

Otherwise, it is not poetry, just thought language flowing along, though not devoid of life; logic has deep meaning, too. But this poem to me is meant to be heard until the words become submerged, and felt, inside the hollows of the self. When its words go back down, they shine through reflections, translucent memory mirrors of loosely conjured images, fragments of sound encountered in one's daily life, though an individual's brain, heading toward that place of pre-thought we know to be there in an animal instinctive way.

Travel this lonely road and you will uncover and discover ancient rhythms, but with modern trappings. Sounds rolled off into structure, and although the sense was there, I avoided the curse of imposed thought, not wanting it to collapse. I can see now, after two decades, engaged again in the pleasure of listening, a shape, a form, an outline of life. The birth and command of youth, the shaping of meaning from age, the grind of looking back and accepting the slowing down, the slow-ward stopping towards the end. Life, something sad, a play in five acts, an inescapable constructive of the new technology age.

Modernity is where we live, and that texture of technology living of this new hyperconnected internet age came out full born from 1999 to 2001 in that first draft. An add-on came with business travel to Europe, where I had spent time before living as a college student and post college rambling around and shacking up. The 'detachment' of the EU, of Europeans in general, made me feel the lack of the true crazed energy of American free-wheeling Silicon Valley capitalism.

This poem was about the New World then, what comes of a rudderless king-less land where no one ruled by divine will, and in relation, looking back on life just past middle age, the old world could be seen, a deliberate footstep or two behind; that is why the fourth part I now realize is placed there, to rev up a contradistinction. The three parts before, then the fifth after, reflects what became of the New World of no safety net, crazed energy, visions of land grabs, developments, birthing of subdivisions and slavery, something sinister and something shining, unlimited dreams if you grab them, and if you don't, you feel dejected like you aren't fully living. A place to be expanded and torn apart. Dreams crush you, secret nightmares have their own shadows. America.

Americans needed a song beyond the sixties and the beatnik scribblings that sang during my father's college years, who is now gone. For me, the eighties and nineties when I formed consciousness of self was not the dream of flower power and peace, penance and diversity embracing. That something was beyond disco freedom of a sexual revolution that devolved passed AIDS which crushed it. The song was sadder maybe, the death of the eighties electronica synth music began to stumble beyond the free love revolution, but into where it couldn't yet be imagined. Freedom of words for all, liberty and justice of anger for all, for everyone to chant in their own pent up twitter feed way, was a just a dream, but readying to be birthed in the gestation Reaganesque period before the internet started to crackle.

Every bit of pent-up magic of language deserved to be felt by all in a swirling tangle of one's own dreams that was preparing to be unleashed. Wires were connecting over circuits, personal computers lashed together, thoughts became giddy as they digitized, passed along the wires of the early internet in sizzling staticy noise of modems hooking up.

I felt it even if it didn't have the words yet. It knew know what was coming: The Unleashing. The promise of no longer following. Of each individual uncaging the self at the lowest levels. Mankind's thoughts were discussed and diatribed over ivory tower harangues above the commoner for centuries. People said people talked freely, but for centuries the words were controlled by scribes hunched over medieval texts, copying them until Guttenberg's press came to the aristocrats who could set up pamphlets free from state controlled religious texts and edits. The printing press was personal, the word of Ben Franklin deciding to get the word out that The King is Dead, we are now Free, America the Dream is birthed. Every member of society can give voice and can give power to the government. It was Common Sense in The Age of Reason. But the people were not yet used to rising up in words. The schools were formed, all individuals could free their own thoughts, the state gave every one room school house books.

Humanity still grew, learned, the basic Industrial Age Machine had to have human hands to stamp out metal car parts, steam engine panels, railroad tracks. Movement was created, cross country freedom driving beyond the horse could now go coast to coast. Thoughts became freer, universities more expansive, every G.I. post-World War II could get a job or education, or escape their past repression, as the Great Migration meant blacks could go forward out of the South again in waves, to the north and east looking for regular acceptance and chances.

But dreams take generations, and the connecting of highways by ground are still slow travelers of words as cars must carry them. Escape. We could all have it. Every American by phone wire could speak state to state, and, if luck, country to country. But when those pathways of wires could carry more than chatty sounds, digital ideas, digital mutterings, the birth of the internet—that, that was the real promise of America.

Every wingnut struggling with anger alcohol issues could try to wrangle out their pain of individual selfhood, grasping at personal meaning, not just on bulky computer business box, but on a clean black slab that could be held into the hand or slipped into a pocket. My first notes came on a Palm Pilot with a foldup keyboard, precursor of the iPhone to come.

Now, the thoughts just ravel wireless around the world, screamed rantings of lunatics are the freeing of every voice, voices that are scratchy and hard to hear for those used to eloquence and refined control of printing presses for centuries. Those at the base, the button, their hands being now freed from the closed down factories where they push a bottom on a twenty-ton metal press stamping out parts into car panels could now use those hands to pull out a pocket machine that wraths their own unkempt thoughts, even if only mimicry, into comment sections, social networks, twitter storms of rage.

The scholars may cringe, but involvement and engagement by all is the only solution to freedom and justice for all. It is an eventuality, a realization that grinds on now, with contributions of ugliness recorded on screen captures. America gives that democracy voice to all. Social evolution is now an unleashed internet entrapment of complete engagement. Dark tendencies emerge into light only when we all have flashlights. There are layers of meaning, layers of emer- gence, dreams of all color and expressions, contradictions and bendings in every breath.

Civility comes only through separation of each. We are a mass of emergence disentangling with only the agreement that what we want as individuals is what we should freely pursue as long it doesn't harm another. Others are invited into our room, come to engage of their own free will; they can agree to enter, consent, and leave when ready, making you stand alone in that room again, clicking away on your machine, without a safety net. Any thought is free to own.

The future is ugly because there is no unity, only ever deepening discord that comes with further individuation. Now we are all on the edge. The center did not hold.

Yet there is something else at play, I admit. Something there below it all, an individual and collective journey to face something else. A religious overtone without religion, an unknown always there between us all, behind and before us, standing before the Gates.

December 2021

PART THREE
EXCESSED POEMS

THE BOOK OF THE POEM

Children don't understand it when it is just real,
The words simple, they are just what they are.

But then a turn happens,
A phrase maybe gets turned around, goes missing,
A thought that was finished loses a word, signaled by a comma,
The sign of hesitation.

The mark is a gap, and the gaps many
sprinkled throughout life.
Small things that can not be regained,
miniature black slits of time, evened out by course events,
Disappeared into the storyline of our
Narrative we know to be whole. Adults.

We cannot have blackness behind us, too.

In our lives,
this is how the language works.
Real simple, with pauses so small
We forget they are gone.

SCRAPS OF LANGUAGE

The crushing fortitude of deep success
Emerges from a broken dream.
Scraps of language slow us down
Bending our intent.

Dream now. It's over.
There is no alive.

There nothing like the streets to unravel your fists upon.

I am that dark place you go to.

Long hope falls in a silent rain,

An outpouring of emotion
always dreaming on…

THE GRATITUDE FRIEND

I would have made it.
If you hadn't blocked my way
with your helpful smile,
that continues inside me
deep into the night,
long after the silence ends

in the far reaches of my dreams.

ALMOST PRAYER

We pray until the lights go out

Years are condensed into moments
And turn into thoughts without reason.

Then the thick spinning takes its toll,
Like a death spiral twisting my head into a fiery knot.

The Dark Lord says whispers of silence:
There is no pain without suffering. There is no violent self without deceit.

Slowly you realize it is there, far off, with no movement or vibration, lurking, somewhere in the recess where the eyes fail: it is sound.
It says: it is I, your master:
I will take you to places of no importance—
a leafless tree on an abandoned prairie,
A burnt out barn with charred roof beams,
A lifeless cave with no echo sitting in the dark for no one—
And return you to exactly nowhere in your mind.

It goes on all night, which now doesn't end.
We pray until the lights inside us are extinguished.

IN DIFFICULT TIMES

If I am somewhere
I'll stay there until it ends.

As the light continues
receding into the future,
broken promises crash
like my dilapidated truck
I had been forced to sell.

I'll be left here as long as I can,
until something moves.
Due to my own admittance
that metal beast that gave so much had dragged on too long.
The hardship.

You can now escape out the back door,
and read a book in the sunlight
until they catch you.

TESTIMONY

And that's how we were left
Struggling along the darkness.

You understand,
Nothing remains in stillness.

There it is:
The great silence you'll never hear
Rumbling in the darkness like a thunderous train
Pulling away from you.

Faint whispers go unturned,
Not strong enough to take to the wind.

Even flight is cancelled.
Just the idea of it is now too repulsive.

But we still walk hand in hand,
Waiting for the day.

Don't we?

Made in the USA
Monee, IL
04 November 2026

67379464R00022